Vagabonds Vol. 3 Issue # 1 2014

EDITOR-IN-CHIEF: Weasel

ASSISTANT EDITOR: Valdon Ross

ASSISTANT EDITOR: Emily Ramse

Vagabonds is an independent anthology that is published twice a year. It is published through Weasel Press.

If you would like a copy of the magazine, you can order one from the Managing Editor at hitchingpoets@hotmail.com.

Vagabonds: Creative Arts Anthology is a non-profit based magazine and runs solely off the support of its readers, authors, and artists. To find out how you can help keep Vagabonds going, email the managing editor at hitchingpoets@hotmail.com

If you would like to be considered for our next issue, please visit our website to see when we open up again.

http://www.vagabondsink.com

http://www.facebook.com/vagabondwriters

http://www.twitter.com/vagabondwriters

http://tmnt802.wix.com/weaselpress

http://www.facebook.com/weaselpress

Featured Artists

Andrea Rose

Fabio Sassi

Grace Mack

Jessi Schultz

Kai James

Karen Boissonneault-Gauthier

Loren Kantor

Featured Writers

Anna Booher

Bill Vernon

Charlier Hunter

Charlie Stern

Chia Chan-Mo

C. R. Resetarits

Debra Bonier

E. M. Cooper

Hannah Gordon

Jane Hertenstein

J. J. Steinfeld

John Hunchak

John Grey

Kat Lewis

Kayla Conway

Kieran

Laura Kitzmiller

Morgan Christie

Phil Lane

Regina Murray Brault

Sendokidu

Simon Hibberd

Steve De France

Valentina Cano

William Tribell

Muses of the vast emptiness,
In your honor, we present this offering of artistic creation. May you continue to inspire and
move us beyond will and awe. Fill us with wonder and guide our imaginations to the nectar
of knowledge. Show us a realm beyond wonder, takes us with you into the nether regions of
space, dance with us in the trails of stardust, give us a taste of your sweet honey so that we
might capture and express, through what we create, a glimpse of the divine within the
profoundly ordinary.

Greetings!

My friends, it is in this spirit that I would like to welcome you to the first issue of the
third volume of Vagabonds: Anthology of the Mad Ones. I first joined Weasel as an
editor of Vagabonds for the second issue. Shortly afterwards, we were joined by Em
Ramser. As the editing staff, we work together to the select the best works submitted to
us. We each bring our separate tastes and passions to this magazine with the hope that
you will be as equally captivated by the art as we have been. Each issue develops its
own flavor and character, highlighting the diversity of our submissions and the craft of
each artist. There are many things we consider and look for in the art we wish to share.
For me, I look for the works that bring something alive within me, that move me in some
way; works that evoke a physical response in my being, and not just some fanciful
daydreams or moments of splendor. It is an organic process that creates each issue, and
somewhere along the way a theme begins to emerge. The theme is not something we
plan, but rather something that is revealed in the art and writing that comes to us. We
simply arrange the selections in a way to amplify the experience, an initial impression
unfolds into a journey of mood, texture, and sensation. It is awe-inspiring to see how the
work that comes to us self-organizes and circumambulates around such themes.
Sometimes directly, at other times, tangentially, there is a thread running through the
collective mind which expresses itself in abstract ways such as this. It fills me with awe
and wonder, and the art contained within this issue, selected from submissions received
from all over Earth, is one such expression of this shared mind and communal
experience of being human.

And so, my friends, I welcome you to join our community of artists -- the deranged and
mesmerized, the crafty and the budding, the genius and the insane, the ordinary and the
exceptional, those in the spotlight and those unseen, the loud and the boastful, the
contemplative and the visionary, the dystopian and the romantic -- the Mad Ones. Join
us as we howl through the streets and the ages.

May you, my friends, continue to be inspired.
Cover the Earth in your art and love.

~ Valdon Ross

"Some people never go crazy.
What truly horrible lives they must lead."

— *Charles Bukowski*

Everyone Is Going To Misgender Me At My Funeral

Charlie Stern

If I die violently,
The news will say,
"One female dead in gruesome homicide/
Gruesome car accident/
Gruesome lion attack."
The paramedics will cut open my clothes
And judge my vulva

Without giving him the opportunity
To introduce himself.
My parents will dress me up
In a green cotton dress
That I rarely wear,
And they'll ignore my wishes to not be embalmed –
Have you ever read
"The Embalming of Mr. Jones"?
Shit's fucked-up –
And they'll insist on an open casket
Because that's what we do
In our family.

And, of course, I fully expect
That my parents will outlive me.
I just hope my mom
Doesn't have to discover my body,
Like if I overdosed at home
And couldn't be roused in the morning.
"Bipolar woman found dead
In apparent suicide."

And all of you will line up
To tell your stories of how
"She" was so funny.
"She" was so nice.
"She" didn't exist and never will.
If I were alive,
I'd make a hack joke, like
"Excuse me, 'she' is my mother;
Call me Charlie."

NINEFINGERS
Kieran

Withershins,

Poor old roots,

Clad in morphine, decked out in doped out,

Ninefingers,

Poor thing.

Poor thing had to be put to sleep,

Had to slip,

In a word, had to drop leaves,

Into a codeine whirlwind -

All teeth, words,

No bones.

Sitting in a rambling joint,

    brambles

Smoke rolls off the walls, we're moving,

       thorns torn from fingernails

Someone's playing jazz

But I don't

really

like jazz.

People sit huddled in toilets,

    hiding blue flowers in the ash.

Dodge the inspector, do coke off keys, are we moving?

 i think we stopped a while ago.

Withershins,

Dying tree,

Gave her a little morphine,

Ninefingers,

Poor thing,

Someone strung her up -

Lost her teeth, no words,

No bones.

Just a smile.

Church Street Market Place

Regina Murray Brault

The woman with the orange crew-cut
holds a blank book to her face. She scans
invisible lines with her black painted nails,
squints over her wire-rims at another
flower-child whose Siamese cat has balanced
itself across her gauze-draped shoulders.

The cat-woman bare foots the bricks
scattering her brown pills as if they were bird-seed –
her red-rimmed eyes watching the patrolman
watching her.

The reader spreads her belongings across the bench
she claims, and returns to her hiding place
behind empty pages.

When my friend pokes my ribs
with her elbow and asks me to define
normal, I consider pointing to a young
mother walking her child on a wrist-leash
but my fingers are held down by the car keys
protruding like small daggers from between
my knuckles -- I have no answers.

Untitled
Jessi Schultz

Steel Rain in Singapore

John Hunchak

The crackle of an old man's dentures has become the death rattle of these narrow Singapore streets. He sits in between two piles of rubble with his old drinking buddies, in front of the bank with the big clock, the one that hasn't stopped burning since day one. It was the first thing I remember catching fire, and its ashes will be the last to wash over this city, I'm sure of it. It's hard for me to understand how they can sit there in lawn chairs, while I gotta dart from building to building in body armor that weighs well over forty pounds and has me sweating fucking bullets. It's just factions that run this place now. These assholes all want a piece of ya. You learn quickly to sleep with one eye open, or else you gotta learn to wake up with a knife twisted deep in your gut. I like to stay on the West end mostly; the worst we got around here is that Feminist cult. The Fems kinda got it in for me. I had a cousin with a history of sexual assault, and by god's good graces we share a bloodline and a surname. He got it real bad when they hauled him in, and I mean real bad. I never particularly liked the guy, he was a disgusting pig, and can't deny I woulda rather enjoyed killin' him myself, so when I heard how badly they did him I lit up a ratty dried up Cuban to celebrate. See they got one big ol' fella in their company, and we call this ruthless bastard Rocko. Rocko stands about 6'7" and I'd put him down around two-hundred and eighty somethin' pounds. I got no idea how he fits in with that lot, but I do know what they use him for. When the Fems get their dainty hands on a man with a record like my unfortunate cousin they like to have a little fun. I'm not going to go too much into detail, but some big crowds come together to watch Rocko give these gutless sons o' bitches a taste of their own medicine if you know what I mean, and I can hear their hootin' and hollerin' from miles away. You can probably hear the screams of the victims too if you got a real good ear, hell everyone's heard the legend of Rocko's member. I got a poison concoction that Quick Johnny cooked up for me in his makeshift lab down at the junkyard in case I ever get caught by any savages.

Just yesterday I had an encounter with those Satan fuckers. I walked outta the parkade I was stayin in the other night when there they were, listening to death metal and ridin' their stupid lookin' blacked out Harleys like always. "Fresh meat boys!" the head of the pack licked his chops. "Join or die motherfucker!" Another one of their goons shouted. I just kept my head down and kept walkin. The dirty girl of the pack strolled up to me, she was wearing a kiss t-shirt and smelled like death, cock and cigarettes. "I'll fuck you real rough if you come with us" she giggled and bit her lip. Her hand was rested on my right shoulder, I stopped walkin. "Is that so?" I inquired "Hell yeah, I'll ride til dawn baby." What she didn't realize is that the fastest hand in the West end didn't need to get laid, the fastest hand in the West end didn't want to hail Satan, he just wanted some wheels. Death metal wasn't my thing anyways, it's got no soul.

Naturally her head was the first to go. I wasn't used to pullin' the trigger from the left hand, so the recoil caught me off-guard, but steel nerves recover quick. The punks tried to turn heel and run, but this revolver carries six and she was conceived to rattle 'em off into the spines of devil worshippers. The lead pierced through the carnage to stop the would be escape artists. I walked through the blood of my enemies towards my prize. I slipped on a leather jacket, and picked the bike up from off the pavement. The sun was starting to set, and someone would have heard the commotion. I turned the keys in the ignition and pointed myself towards the coast.

A Trip, a Dream

Chia-Chan Mo

Taipei. The humid Taipei. The scooter-crammed Taipei. The cars and the scooters were not tired, not yet, of declaring their occupancy over the slippery ground; there came again the crescendo of horns. Aggressive stares were exchanged between the drivers and the riders. It was 11:24 P.M. I was in the middle of a short break from the army. Everyone around the world was looking forward to the coming of tomorrow, but not me.

Tomorrow brought us a new year, 2013; tomorrow also brought the end of my short-lived freedom. The fireworks started, and the fireworks ended. The once highest building in the world, Taipei 101, was turned into a monolithic candle before the fluorescent HAPPY NEW YEAR shining glaringly up in the air. The three words didn't fill my heart with hope. Still, the fireworks were beautiful, but what I felt was all the nothingness it produced. Edward was with his girlfriend; Yvonne was with her girlfriend. I was alone. I followed the crowd, shoals of people. Or, I was forced to follow them. The metro station was two hundred meters away. They had homes to go back to, and I had a training camp.

I left the crowd, went to a 24-hour café, and booked a flight ticket with my laptop. I then bought a Lonely Planet at the bookstore that was also open 24-hours. The distance between the book tightly held in my hand and the flight ticket digitally stored in my email box was eight months and eleven days. During those eight months and eleven days, seven months and two days would be spent in the military camp, the rest in Taipei, before I would print out the digital ticket for actual use, to realize those pictures and the routes suggested in the book.

Date of departure: 12th August 2013.

Every day I would steal a bit of time wedged between one task and another in the army. The stolen time would be stored in the book. I remember on the last day of my service, when packing my personal belongings and ready to leave for good, I took the Lonely Planet out of my allocated cabinet for the last time, somewhat ritualistically. I admired the book. The time spent on this book was so precious: the brevity of the stolen time, bit by bit. One of the facts I had learnt from those precious moments was my destination's population: 1.3 million. The population of that entire county was only half of that of Taipei, the city I lived in. I came to realize: the distance between the here of my whereabouts and the there of my destination was not only eight months and eleven days. It was much more than that.

So, when the digital ticket was finally printed out and wedged between the time-laden pages of the Lonely Planet that was still held in my hand as I waited to check in at the airport, I still didn't know what to expect. Then, I finally arrived in Estonia.

Tere! there came again. Their greeting sounded crispy and brisk, finished with a minim rest. I was on a small Estonian island, Muhu.

Tere! said the Russian-Estonian chef, dressed in a white frock, who came to the bus stop to take me up to the farmhouse, situated in the western top of the island, literally a stone's throw away from Koguva Village.

The village was peaceful, and the farmhouse I lived was too. Among the main building, the fishnet shed, the storehouse, the sauna cabin and the camping site that the farm encompassed, there were only me and the chef, who's English was barely communicable.

I didn't know where to pay for my stay, and the chef was more than insouciant.

Circling around the island, I often marvelled at the sparseness of human activities. I felt that I was either at the very fringe of the world or at the centre of it. The island either detached itself from the world or was the only attachment of it. No one was around. No horn was ever heard. Forest was everywhere. Only a few roads, most of them not asphalted, endeavoured to entwine themselves among the forests and wetlands, frequently in vain. The roads often stopped at some point, abruptly.

There was a boathouse, its walls painted with the colour somewhere between yellow and orange. Later I figured out it was a traditional Muhu colour. The front of the house read restoran. I dismounted, walking to its tangerine door, and was greeted with another Tere, along with a curious stare, a pair of pale blue eyes.

"Usually it won't be pitch-dark until eleven," said the blue-eyed waiter during our intermittent conversation about the weather. His words encouraged me to cycle further. When I was devouring the sült (jellied meat), my feet were already anxious. I wanted to see more of Muhu. I left the restaurant with a phrase that I had just learnt from the chef, my lips still greasy, Tänan!

Thank you.

At around nine thirty, I was cycling back to the farmhouse from Pädaste, another village located at the south-east. Fifteen minutes having passed, I knew it was already too late.

The sky was not pitch-dark, as the waiter said it wouldn't be, while what was almost pitch-dark was the forest. The trees formed a tunnel, soaringly high and hysterically long. Everything was turned into a silhouette: vague, capricious, and wild. Thousands of trees had a communal obsession with the sky that verged on monomania. They devoured all the things the sky gave. I could see no light. It was not only dark; it was wildness. I then remembered what the Russian-Estonian chef said when I patted her Rottweiler, "here, big dogs, because forest animals."

I was a blatant intruder in this dark wildness, and probably also a very weak one. The skyless night went on, on and on. Trees were still around me, and above me. These trees, the barks, and the dark were all bewitching.

So was the wind. It went on and on. The wind was the exertion of my feet on the pedals, the bicycle's murmuring, monotonous and soporific. It had been a while before I came to be aware: I, tired of cycling, as if bewitched, had been unconsciously looking for a spot to snuggle down among the trees and the animals, to wait for the coming of tomorrow. I slowed down. And finally, I stopped and dismounted. The grass stopped rustling, then it started again as my feet squelched through. I plumped down by a tree, and among all the strange dreams, I fell asleep.

I found myself back on the last night of 2012. Taipei 101's fireworks were beautiful. Edward was with me, so was Yvonne. Everyone around the world was looking forward to the coming of tomorrow, so was I. The three words HAPPY NEW YEAR, aglow, filled me with hope, so I made a wish. I murmured to myself: set me free, as free as sleeping among the trees.

Out of Tracks #1
Fabio Sassi

Love Shack

E.M. Cooper

She's seen better days. Splintered boards and crooked poles were her world.

Those lecherous eyes ogled her artless form as she bent

their imaginations and asked one lucky man,

'What's your pleasure?'

She couldn't hear his answer when he flashed his stack

and made it rain.

The howling overpass rattled their shack all night long.

Chocolate Covered Dreams

Debra Bonier

i watch him sleep.

long, brown limbs sprawled in vagrant disarray,

like warm dark chocolate poured over vanilla sheets.

i breathe deeply of the air perfumed by our love,

my body clenching in readiness to taste his sweetness again,

i remember that the greedy grow fat and lazy,

sighing, I roll over and close my eyes to sleep,

dreaming of chocolate sundaes.

Romanceness

Charlie Stern

"I love/adore/worship you with all my heart,"
You shirtlessly gasped
As you swept me up
In your manliness,
Your arms like strong, cologned vines,
Making me feel dominated
And swoony.

I forever cherish
Our walks on the beach/our
Candlelit dinners/your
Perfect adherence
To the hegemonic masculinity script.
You really know how to
Treat a lady.

Ours was a doomed love affair.
We were too attractive/deep/tragic
To be together,
Doomed by war/circumstances/tragedy.
We were ripped apart
Like something
That has been ripped apart.

My days/nights/weekends are filled with
Sighing over you
And our perfect little daughter
That never was.
She would have looked so good
In all these outfits I've already bought her.

Blankets of Ink and Lube Oil

Charlie Hunter

There are things we just don't talk about anymore

Nobody talks about romance these days

Romance not like love or fucking

But true blue romance

True romance is like the siren of Greek literature

We don't believe in the siren

Despite the fact that sirens are screaming at us

Howling and belching their obnoxious noise

Polluting the air with squealing lights and tones

The only solace is the relentless cold quiet

The late nights and early mornings

Stranded in the dead of Winter

Even in this quiet you can hear them

Off in the distance out in the city

Like the howling of wolves the sirens they grow

Like the baying of hounds louder and louder

Coming closer and closer until they knock on the door

Closer and closer until they twist the ears

Closer and closer until they burrow in the mind

Taking up residence like hissing cockroaches in an old boot

So say farewell to romance

The lost art

The last art

True romance like silence in this world

Will never rest in peace

It's just dead.

The Killer
Grace Mack

Cubist Lovers

C. R. Resetarits

The setting is Clovis Sagot's gallery -- a clown's apothecary recast as artistic alchemy. There the faux Egyptian figures under the Picassos are a wry reflection of Rousseau's sales pitch: "Greats of our time--you Egyptian, the Modern mine."

Our hero is just back from the Valley of Kings to hawk his amulets and ancient fake things when a lovely girl stumbles in at the jester's door. She moves like a crane, dark plume, oddly balanced yet plumb. He notes absinthe fumes and a licorice tongue skimming shamrock lips. She weaves, sighs and sings, "How brilliant your charms lined up in a row."

He turns his best smile, best barker's lurk, and contemplates dipping his mesmeric quill into her unctuous ink.

"So delicate and rare. In moonlight they dance; in sunlight spin. Have you a window from which to display? A candle-lit niche – with your beautiful face – a halo of wonder, almost. Come, touch, know, guess their secrets, their weight.

She takes an amulet into her hand, face flushing, slant eyes glazed with effort, and then she drops it into the pocket of her coat, flashes an empty palm, smiles, walks away.

Our boy is pleased. Often after he spots her in town. She is shy, sly. She touches her pocket with fingers as small and delicate as beguiling white lies. He follows, he paints, he captures her elements but not her heart: gold eyes, emerald mouth, and a lovely black-scarlet slash of secrets.

Jack Kerouac
Loren Kantor

Marylou
Hannah Gordon

The busy streets beep below the balcony our legs are dangling from. We could easily fall, plummet to our deaths at any minute, but I think that's why we're shaking and giddy, grabbing each other's hands and twisting our fingers together. God, we feel so alive tonight, don't we?

You're touching my face with the hand that isn't intertwined with mine. You're careful to not graze my cheek with your cigarette, and you only pull your hand away long enough to take a drag, then it's right back where it's supposed to be.

It's only eleven P.M., but we're drunk already—drunk off cheap beer that we stole from your roommates; drunk off each other's promises that we know won't survive in sobriety. We don't care, though, because we have each other running through our intoxicated veins. Every time I breathe, I'm breathing you in, and I swear I've never felt so high. I never want to come down.

For now, we're frozen, high above our small little city, which always feels so big until we take a step back and up to the balcony. Right now, everything is small and beautiful. Our small hectic city that swallows us whole as soon as our feet touch the ground is really quite lovely when you're floating high above it.

"I never want to go back down," you say suddenly, echoing my very thoughts, as though you're there in my head with me, existing simultaneously next to my consciousness.

"I think I would miss you, even if I had never met you," I tell you, staring down at the ant-like people pushing their way through the street to their beds, their lover's beds, the bar, the party, the mirror. None of them look up and see us. They're trapped.

You don't respond, and for the first time all night, your hand isn't on me, but rather in your own lap. The cigarette is gone now.

I'm still drunk but my veins are cold, when you respond, "You shouldn't say such grandiose things. People may believe them."

"What would you rather me say?"

You shrug, and I hear the click of the lighter, again. Surely you've smoked half a pack already tonight, but who am I to judge with all the drinks I had before? I drank them to placate my nerves, which are always on fire whenever you look at me. You smoke when I say grandiose things. We feed into each other's addictions. Dangerous, all-consuming, fire.

"I'd rather you didn't say anything. I'd rather there be silence than for you to fill it with words you don't mean."

You take the first drag, which is always the best. I fold my hands politely in my lap, and suddenly the world below seems to rise up to meet us. We've been gone for too long. It had to remind us who we are, down there.

"But I do mean them," I say quietly, almost a whisper. The honking of a car horn almost drowns me out.

"Dammit. You always have to say things to push me over the edge, don't you? Why can't we just be here, without you complicating it?"

"Complicating it?"

Your hands run raggedly through your messy hair. Your eyes are red.

"Don't make me this irreplaceable force in your life. Don't make me this cemented piece. And you sure as hell should not make me so elemental that you could miss me without even knowing me. Jesus, you shouldn't even miss me ever."

"But I—"

"No, you don't."

We sit in silence for several minutes, and suddenly the closeness I felt to you earlier, when you kissed my lips and it felt like you had for centuries, as though in every previous lifetime we had found each other on this very night, was completely gone.

Suddenly, those very lifetimes felt as though they were in between us. Like all the different versions of ourselves were pushing us apart.

Earlier, when you opened the door, it felt as though we recognized each other for the first time. You smiled, and I felt it inside of me. Surely you felt it too?

We drank, and you told me about the time your father told you he was proud of you. We drank, and I told you about the first time I looked in the mirror and didn't like what I saw. You kissed me and promised that you could never look at me and feel like that. Because all you saw was everything you wanted. We got drunker and madder and began to talk about everything we wanted to do. We decided to leave—not now, but soon, maybe even tomorrow. We'd go west—everyone went west. It'd be like all the stories we read when we were in high school and craving love and adventure, and that's exactly how we felt now. You could be Dean Moriarty, and I'd be your Marylou. I didn't think you'd ever read the book, but I didn't have the heart to tell you.

You wanted to get out. You didn't feel good enough here, so you figured you'd make a place where you could. I'd never felt good, no matter where I went, but if I were with you, maybe I'd try. I didn't know what had gotten into us. It was as though we were just finally opening our eyes.

I think you're sober now. Your cigarette is gone, and you stand to leave. I think, for a moment, you're going to leave me, but you reach a hand out to pull me up.

I'm cold when we go inside, but the feeling is familiar, and all of this makes too much sense, because cigarettes are only beautiful in poetry. Your cigarette smoke, in my hair, on my hands, soaked into my flesh, is only beautiful in the poems I write—late at night, cold tea in my hands, clock ticking away. But right now, I can't wait to get home and wash you out of my hair.

I guess I'm more your Marylou than either of us intended.

You kiss my cheek before I leave, but it's not the same. It's not anything, really. Just two pieces of skin touching by mere chance and nothing else. I walk home in the cold, back on the streets that swallow me whole. Everything is so big—I want it to stop. I want to be back on that balcony. I want to swallow my grandiose words, or, at least, make you believe them.

You grab a beer with your roommates and laugh at some dumb joke they say. You're planning on leaving in a week for the west, wherever. I go home and curl up in a bed as empty as the promises you made me, and I feel more myself than ever.

Emily's Scrapbook

Anna Booher

Emily woke up to a pain in her mouth. The blackness around her told her that it was the middle of the night. Her tummy rumbled under the sheets.

She slumped up to sitting position, and the insides of her hips felt that familiar sharp throbbing under her pajama bottoms. She stared apathetically at the tuft of hair that had fallen onto the blanket in front of her, looking like a dull orange rodent. It was bigger than the last one. Hungrily, she snatched it up quickly and balled it into her fist, darting to the living room where she had left her scrapbook.

Kiss today goodbye...the sweetness and the sorrow.

Emily lived now in a space of five rooms, a kitchen with nothing but a table where food sometimes appeared...sometimes. A bathroom was across from it with a sink, a tub, and toilet, and two bedrooms—one for a new little girl and one for an old little girl. A living room also served the purpose of a practice room with only a sofa, a coffee table, and a television so that the girls could watch recordings of themselves. Mirrors also hung on every wall. Possessions were given to little girls who had talent. Back when Emily had talent, she was given a scrapbook, and now Emily needed it.

Emily darted to the sofa. The other new little girl, Amelie, was rehearsing in here, but Emily needed that scrapbook. Emily balled herself into a hunched position onto the sofa, as she quickly took her pink and light blue scrapbook off of the coffee table. She quickly stuffed the orange discolored tuft of hair into one of the little plastic bags she had sewn into each one of the pages, for times like this when she had lost something. She did not want Amelie to see. She should have been more careful. She should not have left her personal things around, not for the new little girl to see.

If Amelie had taken a peek inside of Emily's scrapbook, Emily hoped the new little girl had only seen the first few pages. The pages she used to show the other girls when she herself had been a new little girl and had been taken out to meet other little girls with the same talents—pictures of her in the light blue bathing suit. Her hair when it was long, auburn, and pretty.

Now Amelie was here. Food appeared more often for Amelie than it did for Emily, because Emily could stand to lose the flab off of her puffy tummy. Emily also had to give most of her clothes to Amelie, because Amelie could make more use out of them.

Emily watched as Amelie stood on her perfectly straight toes, her perfectly brunette ringlets bouncing onto Emily's old light blue bathing suit. She was watching a recording of herself.

Wish me luck the same to you... It's as if we always knew...

Emily absently fingered the tuft of hair through the plastic bag. She wondered if Amelie's hair would start falling out one day too. Emily flipped through more of the back pages where there were no pictures, just little bags with hair and yellowed baby teeth.

We did what we had to do...

Amelie twirled and pirouetted on her toes, her fingers extended like she was drinking tea. She kept singing softly, trying not to wake Emily who was supposed to be asleep in the next room. Emily thought of her own voice that was so sore right now and sounded like a squawking crow whenever she tried to sing. Her feet were too beaten and callused to look pretty on her toes. Her tummy would stick out of that blue bathing suit.

Amelie twirled around once and stopped, seeing Emily watching her. Her perfect mouth made a sweet "oh." Emily told her that she was beautiful, because she was. She closed her scrapbook and took it with her back to bed.

In the morning, the pain in Emily's mouth produced a small white tooth—her last baby tooth. She reached for her scrapbook at the side of her bed.

Won't forget, can't regret what I did for love.

Amelie twirled and pirouetted on her toes, her fingers extended like she was drinking tea. She kept singing softly, trying not to wake Emily who was supposed to be asleep in the next room. Emily thought of her own voice that was so sore right now and sounded like a squawking crow whenever she tried to sing. Her feet were too beaten and callused to look pretty on her toes. Her tummy would stick out of that blue bathing suit.

Amelie twirled around once and stopped, seeing Emily watching her. Her perfect mouth made a sweet "oh." Emily told her that she was beautiful, because she was. She closed her scrapbook and took it with her back to bed.

In the morning, the pain in Emily's mouth produced a small white tooth—her last baby tooth. She reached for her scrapbook at the side of her bed.

Won't forget, can't regret what I did for love.

Fig
Kayla Conway

Purple and brown,

Stretching,

Pregnant,

I opened it

Devouring its tentacle seeds,

Its flesh.

Finding worms

And rot.

Sunshine and Hedgehogs
Andrea Rose

Everlasting
Sendokidu

Sleeping dreams wisp away, a
Cavern's secret trove beckoning.
Legends old enkindle weary
Hearts, and adventure's sought over.

Taverns' glistening jewels
Spin the golden spiel further,
Reaching high above onto
Perilous peaks of fire.

Wakes of the past soon seethe through
Youthful bellies, one such
Churned towards the merciless gambit
Drenched in kingdoms' treasure.

Sword held out, the Hero
Walks the trodden path through
Glades unkempt of man, a
Lush undisturbed with beauty.

Hoary mountains quivering,
Snow pelts down upon the
Wanderer's back as the welkin
Sighs, the journey nearing its close.

Flames spewing forth from out the
Earthly chimney, he enters,
Staggering through darkened
Halls of unknown terrors.

Quaking bellows surge through the
Ground, the room alight in a
Warm glow as a serpent
Large and bold from sleep stirred.

Blade and fang glare down the
Rivals' joust, a wiry
Smile the last remorse as the
Two lay 'way their weapons.

Passing years lead back to those
Humble pubs again, the
Youth of then no longer
Fancied with tales of the elders.

Reminiscing of days long
Gone, a man of age takes
Hold a quelling boy so
Fit to live without his dreaming.

Wrinkled lips locked in a grin, he
Turns the child around, his
Grey eyes shining with a
Light thought lost a world ago.

Pulling out a scale of blue,
Words of desire seep into
Venturous ears while the dragon
Strings along his thread fermenting.

PETA & PROFESSORS & PUSSYCATS

Steve DeFrance

The professor grew fat drinking esoteric wines.

Neighbors inspect him as a potential 4th for bridge.

He despises them their mediocrity & breeding habits---only

nine months respite between litters!

He snarls & eats & drinks & all folks agree

he has a certain bohemian charm for a misanthrope,

but no practical promise as a bridge partner.

The professor stares at his class for 45 minutes

before beginning his lectures on *Euclidean Errors*.

He yearns for spiritual escape; it comes in the shape

of a new black BMW convertible.

Driving home in the crush-hour-traffic

he reasons he can afford $1000.00 payments

since *he isn't breeding.*

He lives without benefit of clergy

with a female attorney--Helen--in a squalid breeding

tract of Post-World-War ll stucco houses.

Helen tethers him there like an ancient sacrificial goat.

Produces food & sex & wine. She wants children.

But the professor holds fast to his no-breeding-rule.

Hence, Helen elopes with the office *ad hoc sperm donor.*

For weeks the professor stays too drunk

to notice a pallid moon flickering across

the seamless rows of housing tract.

One night

deep in his cups---he falls from the porch

landing heavily in the lawyer's Geranium Bed.

There he strokes a bedraggled cat saying,

"My lawyer's gone---off to Paris or Venice

off forth seeking her silken silhouette in the sun."

As the word *off* passes his lips

he slips into a lisping sleep---sliding beneath the foliage.

There he dreampt he slept on a cold hillside

playing bridge with jungle leopards

who had the faces of his neighbors.

The leopards & he ate the neighbor children.

Then, after eating Helen & her sperm donor,

the leopards & he made love on the grass. . .

In the morning--suffering a hangover in the shape of a bison--

the professor is greeted by a hard-jawed woman from PETA,

she inspects his many cat scratches & scars

 & together they pluck fur from between his teeth.

Both feel a quiver of excitement.

Nessie

Phil Lane

I bet old Hemingway's muse was some piece of ass—nice for him. The closest thing I have is this monster I'm married to. She's there waiting for me like a hitman, her beady eyes trained on me like two judgmental pistols. "Writer, my ass," she snickers, arms crossed, a disapproving glare rolling around on her fat face. I look down at the blank page that droops gloomily out of the old Smith-Corona. "I'm going down to Miller's," I announce but she's already upstairs in her armchair chuckling and snorting at some stupid sitcom. She shovels a generous portion of apple pie into her mouth in between wheezy chortles. I'd like to kill her—that'd create some grist for the mill. "How I Slayed the Loch Ness Monster"—now that's a title.

Atchison, this jackoff from down the street, is the only one at the Miller's. I sidle up next to him and we swill beer and talk about man stuff: "my wife does nothin' but bitch, bitch, bitch" and "that's why women have two sets of lips—one to piss with, one to moan with." When I get home, Hamilton, the mailman, is fucking the Loch Ness Monster in the ass. Her gelatinous hocks ripple as he thrusts his scissory body forward into the wretched, mossy abyss. He looks up at me and starts stammering a jumble of half-syllables. I flash him a thankful glance and dash downstairs to the workbench that serves as my writing table. I place my fingers on the keys of the old Smith-Corona dramatically and begin clunking away:

When I get home, Johnson, the mailman, is stabbing the Loch Ness Monster in the gut. Her cellulite wattle swings back and forth like a pendulum. Her arms flail like two elephantine flippers. Johnson looks up at me and starts stammering: "that's why women...two setsa lips...one ta piss with...one...ta moan with." I flash him a grateful glance and a sympathetic smile. The mailman delivers one final cleave and the Loch Ness Monster lies on the floor like a beached manatee, motionless. The steak knife falls to the linoleum with a clang of freedom.

Émigré
Kayla Conway

I was allergic to whores. They spawned like rabbits, morphing into a five-breasted Barbie. She could do every job except impress me.

Afterschool they all procrastinated in their sonic playgrounds: happy, frisky, plastic.

Afterschool I ran home, determined to slaughter my sneezing. So I would: roll some grass, lay back, listen up, tune in, tune out, turn on and fall off the cliff. And I would watch as my life rolled by, a nickelodeon, a silent Technicolor picture show.

Ernest Hemingway
Loren Kantor

Cemetery Visit
J. J. Steinfeld

I pulled my car over and parked in front of the cemetery, the oldest cemetery in the country a plaque on the wrought-iron front gate claimed. I had grocery shopping to do, was on my way to the store before closing, and yet something made me stop here. I've long avoided funerals and cemeteries, going only when I was a child and my parents forced me to attend those of relatives, but that was a lifetime ago, and now I felt compelled to enter this cemetery, which has so many strangers standing and looking at graves or walking among the headstones.

I hear a woman before I see her kneeling in front of a headstone, she wailing, "My child, my child," but she fails at resurrection. Then I hear a nearby voice, but cannot see its source, yet clearly hear its piercing wail, "The bravest soldier," sensing they are words for a buried hero. I see diminutive graves for infants, stately graves for heroes. I don't know if I'm more frightened or confused, but the caretakers catch my attention, as if they might offer me some relief from the voices and graves. I think, *Look, the caretakers work like ants, look, the ants are indifferent to death*, but am afraid to say my thoughts aloud. I want to declare this observation to everyone in the cemetery, to free myself with these words, but I find it impossible to speak. Without warning, my attention is taken from the caretakers: There, a beloved husband and father; there, a beloved brother and son. Revered graves for parents, piteous graves for children, I hope they get the weeds—no births, no wars, in cemeteries, only dark ends, tearful friends, the fearful living viewing the orderly vastness of death, viewing the disorderly prophecies of life. Two voices in unison wail, "She was all alone," and I think, *No longer, silent company...look, the ants are indifferent to death.*

The bawdy talk of the gravediggers, moans the ripped music: *sing, sufferers, sing, sing to the chiselled stones, to the mourners, to the dead*—the mourners and the dead have paid dearly for your concert, but the chiselled stones endure, they require no songs, no cures, yet to the dead all sounds are noise, even silence, especially silence. Tree-lined graves, well-defined resting places, and I am confronted by my mind's assertion: *Only the dead speak wisdom.*

Someone screams, "I miss you," and all turn and share their weariness, then return to their private grief. Coward's death, hero's death, the patient ground welcomes all with an eternal piety...*Look, the ants are indifferent to death.*

A tired gravedigger leans on his shovel; a tired weeping woman leans on her memory...*Look, the ants are indifferent to death.* I wail out something but I cannot even hear myself amidst all the voices and I feel as though I will never be able to leave this cemetery reputed to be the oldest one in the country. I want to think of meaning and purpose and lives lived but my thoughts become trapped in the one inescapable conclusion: *Look, the ants are indifferent to death.*

Another Paradise Lost

Morgan Christie

Characters
Sin, *Lucifer's daughter*
Lucifer, *and or Satan*
Moloch, *a pro-war angel*

Setting
The outskirts of heaven

On the outskirts of said heavenly beyond, only days prior to that inevitable fall that would change his name from Lucifer to Satan; the soon to be fallen angel watches the most alluring woman he has seen basking in the glow of twilight. The seated woman wears a red shawl and is called Sin; springing from Lucifer's own head when he first disobeyed his father. The unnatural act, disobedience, resulted in a piece of the angel separating from the rest of him, creating a daughter if you would, who was created in a similar likeness to Lucifer himself. Enamored by her beauty, Lucifer is in the midst of gazing at Sin from a far as she sets a flame to one scented herb and sucks the life from it as his grisly comrade, Moloch, approaches.

Moloch (*Startling Lucifer*): What are we up to this fine night's eve?

Lucifer (*Annoyed*): Approach me from behind again and we will be up to something far less pleasant Moloch.

Moloch (*Laughing*): Calm yourself Lucifer, it was but a jest. (Moloch spots Sin in the distance and glances around Lucifer's shoulder) Ah, but who is this lovely creature you peer at from the shadows?

Lucifer: Her name is Sin.

Moloch: Indeed. And what a specimen she is, I shall have her.

(*Moloch begins to approach Sin*)

Lucifer (*Lucifer grabs Moloch by the arm and thrusts him back*): You will do no such thing. She was spun from my mind and if anyone will have her, it will be me!

Moloch (*Raising his arms in surrender*): Be easy old friend, I did not know. Have you touched the beauty that is this, Sin, yet?

Lucifer (*Sits*): I have tried, she resists.

Moloch (*Kneels beside Lucifer*): Resists? You speak as though she has been given a choice.

Lucifer: She has been; one so striking, so rich in her wonders and in the depth of her mind deserves a choice.

32

Moloch: Am I hearing the words of our fearless champion, the one bent on leading our rebellion against The Father, or those of a wee babe?

Lucifer (*Angrily*): Watch your tongue Moloch!

Moloch: Alas, there he is. There's the conqueror I've come to know. If only you could speak so harshly to she that rests behind us.

Lucifer: I can.

Moloch: So why not do it?

Lucifer: It is this matter of her stemming from my thoughts, being a portrait of perfection, the mirror to my soul. It seems a dangerous thing Moloch, this utopia, the ability to attain one's grandest desire; the undisclosed result worries me. We thought our father perfect once; we thought heaven our paradise...

Moloch: This is true, but you plan to overthrow The Father and his chosen son, to take this heaven for yourself and the rest of us who follow you. What makes her (*Moloch motions to Sin*) any different?

Lucifer (Slowly standing): Nothing, nothing...

Moloch reveals a slight grin and faintly chuckles before disappearing as Lucifer approaches Sin; he kneels before her and removes the smoking stem from her lips. He takes a wisp. Lucifer puts the stem down and attempts to touch Sin's cheek, she turns away, he tries again, and she rejects him further. He then takes hold of the red shawl she is wearing and attempts to take it from her, she pulls it back. The two rise and struggle to gain control of the shawl until finally, Lucifer rips it from her grasp and Sin falls to the ground. Standing above Sin, Lucifer smells then wraps the shawl around his shoulders and basks in its beauty, before throwing it on the ground and leaving Sin ravished and alone.

Sin: How dare he, how dare he take what was mine for his own. (*Grabs stomach in pain*) Oh, how it hurts! This seed so quickly forming in my womb; even now, its power emanates. When it is born, I will name it Death, and watch it wreak the havoc I already sense. Lucifer will return for it, for Death, to use our child as his greatest weapon. (*Begins to stand*) But I will not give it up, as without me, without this vessel, his supreme power would not be. Without me; he would have nothing, nothing at all.

And so Sin left the confines of heaven, and Death was born.

Monster #9
Kai James

ALPHABET SOUP
John Grey

One letter is a bone, notched
and whitened. Another, a kneecap,
A third, sharp and pointed,
an undisguised chin,
Is that a W made of fingers?
Or a stoic T protecting the breast?
The S clearly holds together
the mixed emotions. And no one
doubts the pelvic Y.

Capitals click and clack
against lower case. The Q dwindles
off, a minor genital, thin as a spider's leg.
Z rules the skull even when X marks the spot.

I knew them for what they are,
useless vassals without the dignity of words,
the cover-up of flesh.
Some are loose. Some stiff
as the drink the round-backed lounging G
always looks like it needs.

You can see them or you can imagine them.
You can sit with me
and name them, one through twenty six.
I don't beat the drum for myself.
Though the spine would be drum-sticks
but for the rigid I.

Happy Place
Valentina Cano

When my hands shake

like ice in tumblers,

I think of the way my mother

presses sheets.

One by one,

tucking corners and folding right down the middle.

That's what I would like to do:

become so thin and tight

I can be stored away,

for future use, in a drawer.

Hunter Thompson
Loren Kantor

Broken Home
Charlie Hunter

Coming from a broken home

Myriad first world problems

Plethora of minuscule trivial troubles

A true dodeca-dilemma drudgery of a life

Always something to complain about

My oven only works on broil

Pizzas and potatoes don't do so well

When the oven doesn't bake

My sink is full of dishes and scum

The pipes are frozen and the heater

Well it sounds like a low-flying Cessna

But with a little motivation and a good day

The heater is fixed as best as can be

It's still loud but a hell of a lot warmer

The pipes have thawed and the water runs

Worn boots stand atop the world for a spell

But it doesn't take long at all

Before the world switches gears

The sink is clogged with grease and slime

The broiler on the oven has retired

And the water heater in the bathroom

Well it is working part-time shifts

At least the water heater has a job.

Pale Ashes In A Porcelain Urn
Regina Murray Brault

A blue-eyed, stone-faced 9 year old boy
walked among men exiting a coal mine.

He grew-up to be a boxer leaning
against ropes, staring at blood-stains
smeared on his Golden Gloves.

In time, he became a front-line soldier
fighting from a foxhole with the red-tipped
bayonet he'd later carry home.
He needed to sell it there, "as is".

Home was where he exhaled the off-white paints
his brushes stroked on someone else's clapboards,
then spit-out dark asbestos from close contact with
torn-shingled roofs.

He covered his mouth with handkerchiefs when
the spots from Black Lungs suddenly appeared
like tar on the burning walls of Hell.

There were few, if any, stained-glass windows
or splintered rainbows coloring his life, only this
hand-full of scarlet rose petals mixed with his ashes

inside the cloud-white porcelain urn we now watch
being lowered and buried in hard Earth on which
he'd proudly followed his even harder path.

Through it all, I still remember most, the color
of those beautiful blue eyes, softly closing when
we hugged goodbye.

Last Ride #1
Fabio Sassi

In the Belly of Time

Bill Vernon

The bus was my metal mother. Outside her the world whistled past like a film on fast forward. I glimpsed what appeared through the windows so briefly, the farms, the houses, the towns, the bad weather, all seemed more dream-like than real.

I'd snuggle a shoulder against the padded wall, my head against the glass, and my mind wandered. I couldn't read. Looking down nauseated me although on the way home I sometimes thought up and jotted down what I called poems, pious reports of God in the trees or on the land. These I had enough sense not to show anyone.

Sometimes I'd sit barefooted, my socks on the seat beside me. Their exposure to air in the hour's drive could dry them. I liked walking through the lawn when it was glistening from heavy dew in the porch light from our house, but wearing soaked socks all day was no good. I liked scaring off rabbits, whose cottontails disappeared in the darkness. I liked hearing cowbells ring as Holsteins foraged in their pasture across the street from us. I liked how the Greyhound stopped with a hiss of brakes, how its doors swished open, how the driver said good morning, took my ticket, and slammed the door behind me.

I liked doing my first dance of the day, holding my texts and notebooks high while swiveling forward deeper inside, avoiding the feet, legs, elbows, and heads that hung out into the aisle from the paired seats on either side, my free hand gripping the metal luggage rack for balance. Dim bulbs lit the obstacles I sometimes bumped, causing a groan.

The passengers were seldom awake, and if they were, we avoided eyes. Looking away was the universal habit. There might be a glowing cigarette in one seat, an open eye glinting from an outside light in another. The air, though, was rich with essences, of perfume, cologne, a recently peeled orange, tobacco smoke, sweat, and sometimes a starkly animal smell. From horses? A farmer on his way to the city?

I'd sit at the very rear and listen to shoes shuffling, clothes rustling, the snoring, coughing, and sniffling. I might yawn myself, but I never slept, too afraid of missing my stop. In Dayton doing that would mean a 13-block hike back to school. Doing it on the return in the evening could mean facing a 20-mile ride home from Cincinnati, assuming I had enough money for a ticket. My eyelids never closed longer than a blink.

I'd look out a window and watch the new dawn or dusk arrive. I never knew the people I traveled with. Anonymity was practiced here. For a few moments together, sitting in the belly of time, we shared a purpose, moving toward and/or away from something. The daily trips connected my heart at home to my head at school, and together they seemed to make me into who I was.

Lubbock Taxi Driver from Roswell

C. R. Restarits

"Me? I'm from Roswell, New Mexico. Yeah, yeah, UFOs and such. Couldn't wait to leave. First time, not so good. Took a bus to El Paso. Seven hours. When I got off, I said, Ok, I guess maybe I'm done with buses. Why I drive a taxi . . . not a bus. Dated this girl from Texas Tech once. She'd take a bus home once a month to Odessa. I told her I didn't ride no bus cause I once rode a bus seven hours to El Paso and she said, Aw, it ain't so bad, and I said, Ok, I guess maybe you like riding a bus. Not me. But I do love traveling. Once drove a semi to Oklahoma to pick up a silo. Stayed at a little motel with a pool. Go out and there's no water in that pool. Go to the clerk and asked, How come there's no water in the pool? Fella says we're fixing to paint it. And I said, Ok, I guess maybe it needs painting more than you need me sleeping and so I quit him and slept in my truck. Another time delivering turbines to St. Louie and visited this riverboat for gambling. Go to play black jack and the dealer says, you're not from around here are you? And I say, No, I'm from New Mexico and she says, Mexico! And I said, No, New Mexico. Between Arizona and Texas, maybe you heard of them. She says Well I knew you weren't from around here. And I said, Ok, I guess maybe you know black jack about here and there. But I do love traveling. Was suppose to do basic training in Fort Hood, Georgia, and right before I was to go they changed it to Fort Bliss in El Paso and I thought, Ok, I guess maybe that's a little bit back asswards cause I'd still like to see a little more Georgia and a little less Texas . . . long as it ain't on a bus. Ha. Lubbock International, m'am. Wish I was going with you."

Sideways and Otherwise
William Tribell

I am just a human being

Quite busy being

With my wagon

Wearily weaving

From rut to rut

Hitched to a wondering star

Turning near to far

Into the irrelative relative

Talent, Genius, Divine

A wink of the eye

Breath

Soul

Joy, gladness

Serenity, madness

Ecstasy

No one knows what they don't know

Many think they know what they know

For sure; safe and secure

Positive

None as strange as folk

The worldwide living doorway tide

When the buses are slow

Some times I see you seeing me

For what I am and what I want to be

I see all of us and you and we

All the many people

All about in plenty

Busy like bees used to be

But people dancing look like fools

To those who can't hear the music

Playing in the background

Soundscape

Step, step, pivot, turn

Just a human

Being

Seeing

Rut to rut

Near to far

I am

Rays of Health

Andrea Rose

Multiple Facebook Personalities

Jane Hertenstein

I don't know when it all started. Fiction is hard to pin down. It begins with an idea and then spirals out of control.

After getting an MFA I spent a year sending out my thesis, a collection of linked stories that were primarily character driven. I wasn't getting any takers. I tried to be upbeat at my Facebook page. Hey! Anyone know of an editor dying to meet a menagerie of halfway house patients? Not everyone in my book is crazy, just slightly off-kelter. Quirky!

Breathe deep, I told myself. I knew I had to cast a wider network net. I checked out books at the library on marketing and promotion, which all seemed to say the same thing: Social media is key.

So I started a Facebook fanpage. I linked it with a Twitter account. Not just me, but about me as an author. I invited my friends to *like. Instead of posting personal stuff, I kept it strictly professional. With every query I sent out I made sure to include links to this fan page.

In the meanwhile I worked on submitting to various literary journals—knowing that publishing credits are like cash in the bank. After having been away from some of the stories for years—a few had been written as an undergraduate—I realized almost all of them needed polishing. More than a spit bath, but a good soak in the re-write tub.

My advisor at the time I was getting my masters was constantly berating me—Get inside your characters. We met every week—usually to reset my compass after an especially grueling critique session. Let's just say the workshop I was in was not based on mutual respect or a generosity of spirit. More like dog eat dog. This one girl, let's call her Kimberly, was always on me about showing and not telling me. Finally I shouted at her: Show me! I swear she was a broken record player that could only play one tune. Which when I said that, she merely rolled her eyes and said that was cliché.

I remember at one point feeling absolutely desperate (sort of like how I feel right now), on the verge of tears or self-mutilation, which I haven't participated in for quite a while, since high school. I called my advisor at home and then drove out to her house. It might've been midnight, or later. We sat in her living room while she talked me down. Finally she asked something that has stuck with me. "What's in your character's purse?" They don't carry a purse, I tried to explain. They use a backpack. "Same thing," she went on. "Tell me details about your character. What's on their bedside stand? What's on their reading list?"

I get it, I shouted. Get inside them!

My advisor smote her forehead as if this should have been obvious. And maybe it was. Ever since I was a kid I've taken the long way around to get someplace. Sometimes I get a little lost along the way. My mother was always happy to point out that I was "different." Well, so are many of my characters. I went home and wrote for five days straight (before finally crashing) a series of "letters" from my characters to me, revealing all their secrets, motivations, the real color of their hair, underneath all those fake highlights and dime store color jobs. We talked for hours.

It was like a reunion. I hadn't realized how much I missed some of the people populating my stories—except for a minor character based on Kimberly that I tacitly killed off in the third story in the book when my main character pushed her off the EL platform onto Addison Avenue into Cubs' baseball traffic. No one had to tell me my main character was drunk; I already knew it when I wrote the scene.

I opened up several new Facebook accounts under my fictional character's names. There were so many blank spaces to fill in: the types of music they listened to, movies and books they liked, where they attended high school and where they worked. Once I finished a section Facebook always wanted more. I downloaded images off the Internet and plugged them into the Timeline. One character from the halfway house got engaged to another patient. He gave her a teddy bear to celebrate and I put up a picture of that. Whenever my characters dined out I took cellphone photos of their extravagant desserts. I had a character that was always posting about her dog—just like Kimberly who I reluctantly stayed in contact with, who was either celebrating her latest book contract or ranting about her poochie-pooch. I had a car run over her dog.

Not Kimberly's but my main character's. I commented at her Facebook page, I told Kimberly to show, not tell.

All in all I started about 30 Facebook pages. It was hard keeping them separate. I was always getting mixed up. In fact it took most of my waking time dealing with all their problems that I had very little time left over for revising.

When I see my therapist every Monday she asks about how my characters are doing, I sigh. The life of an artist is so fractured. Sometimes it seems one big fiction.

Sex and Duck
Steve Hibberd

A Joyful noise flirts from her lips

she leans against the kitchen side

I know exactly what she's doing

But my smile is impossible to hide

Half dressed but fully alive

She bites a lip with lusty eyes

her breasts push against my back

heavy breaths fill my mind

"Dinner will be ruined"

I pretend to protest

As I surrender my arms

and then the rest

Wine and skin find our lips

"A scratch for me a bruise for you"

dinner is over now

but we still bite and chew

Satisfied and content

her hips no longer buck

But her playful voice soon chimes

"We smell like sex and duck"

Friday Night
Kat Lewis

10:35 PM: Head to the boys' dorm with your roommate against your better judgment. Text your boyfriend. Tell him that you'll Skype later. Remember your deck of Dollar Store playing cards. Remind your roommate to bring that water bottle with your school's logo. The one that reeks of apple vodka and regret.

10:42 PM: Meet the guys in their common room. Shuffle the cards. Play Asshole or BS. Laugh. Trash talk. Wait for the right opportunity to say your mother's favorite line, "Bite the pillow. I'm going in dry."

11:15 PM: Put away the cards. Follow everyone into the your closest friend's room. Sit on his Boba Fett bedsheet clad bed. Watch them take shots. Decline a drink. Listen to their toasts: "May our lives be long and manhoods be stiff." Try not to laugh. Watch your roommate smell her water bottle and cough. Smell it against your better judgment.

11:20 PM: Be asked why you don't drink. Remember the time in 11th grade when you played Edward 40 Hands. Remember the panging pain in your head and how heavy it felt the next morning. Remember the cool feeling of your toilet's porcelain against your cheek. Smile and say that you just prefer not to drink.

11:22 PM: Be asked if you're straight-edge. Tell them you don't like that holier-than-thou stigma. Tell them how you roll your eyes at those triple X stay true tattoos and the obnoxious t-shirts that try to look hardcore with the old English fonts and battle ready eagles. Get blank stares. Back paddle and say, "Yeah, I'm pretty much straight edge."

11:30 PM: Go to a party against your better judgment. Dance to the first few songs. Grow tired of the smell of salty sweat and liquor. Sit on the wall. Politely decline the advances of your closest friend because you have a boyfriend back home in Seattle or Milwaukee. Watch him walk away. Watch bodies grind against one another. Watch the speakers quake with each beat of bass. Feel entirely alone.

12:03 AM: Drink what you thought was Country Time Lemonade. Give this college experience a chance. You're older now. How could you make the same mistakes?

12:15 AM: Drink a lot against your better judgment. Dance with that same friend. Get a text from your boyfriend. Don't reply

12:53 AM: The cops arrive.

12:54 AM: Escape out back hand in hand with your friend. His bony fingers feel foreign between yours.

12:55 AM: There's a pitting in your stomach like you've done something wrong. But he makes you giggle and you forget that you feel anything at all.

1:02 AM: Follow your friend to another party against your better judgment. Don't hear your cell phone buzzing in your back pocket.

1:05 AM: Drink more "lemonade". Dance until your arches ache and your knees shake.

1:22 AM: Return to his dorm against your better judgment.

1:42 AM: Play Call of Duty. Take a sip each time you die. Remember too late that you suck at video games.

2:11 AM: Black out.

8:23 AM: Wake up tangled in stiff Star Wars sheets and the smell of booze and boy. Find your clothes and phone. Tip-toe outside.

8:30 AM: Carry yourself on sore legs. Start your first walk of shame.

8:33 AM: Check your phone. Find five missed calls and thirteen texts from your boyfriend.

8:40 AM: Call him back.

9:03 AM: Break his heart.

the unconcealing.
Laura Kitzmiller

the unearthing of diamonds

from the clutter,

the slice of light that hits

the room, golden

peeled off sunshine,

lay bare on the floor--

falling asleep

to a water hymn,

an entrancing beat of rain

and steamed heat, i listen to

the skimming tires on streets,

backcountry roads

and highways,

i'm looking straight between--

as the afternoon sun

turns to dusk.

for you and i

    have suffered much,

    still,

    i do not know

    the meaning of

    enough.

Karen Boissonneault-Gauthier
Blow Your Horn

Who Are Our Contributors?

Andrea Rose

My name is Andrea Thomas. I live as a fruitarian in Southern Colorado and I like to play with my food. You can find more of my fruitography on my facebook page (facebook.com/andrea.rose.9279) where I also list artwork for sale such as photography and photography transferred to canvases. I also paint on occasion and post my paintings there as well. Custom work is also available by request.

Anna Booher

Anna Booher is a twenty-two year old aspiring novelist, songwriter, and short story writer. She is very excited to submit to Vagabonds: Anthology of the Mad Ones. She has been published in publications such as The Rambler and Forte, both publications at Illinois College. She has also been published in The State Journal Register, the Springfield, Illinois newspaper. Emily's Scrapbook is a haunting tale about a young girl who is slowly aging into oblivion. She is being replaced by a younger and prettier version of herself, Amelie. The story takes place as Emily's own body revolts against her as she observes Amelie thriving.

Bill Vernon

Bill Vernon served in the United States Marine Corps, studied English literature, then taught it. Writing is his therapy, along with exercising outdoors and doing international folkdances. His poems, stories and nonfiction have appeared in a variety of magazines and anthologies, and Five Star Mysteries published his novel OLD TOWN in 2005.

C. R. Resetarits

C. R. Resetarits' recent microfiction appears in New York, NANO, The Newer York, and Post Road.

Charlie Hunter

I am just another self-prescribed writer trying to get by. I find myself residing in Oregon, but more often than not I live in my imagination.

Charlie Stern

Born and raised in Massachusetts, with North Carolina connections, Charlie Stern is a vegan, left-handed, feminist, genderqueer radical who will probably end up in prison one day.

Chia Chan Mo

As I'm typing this, I'm 25. With one thing and another, he's now on the train, with a notebook on his lap, going back to his university, the University of Warwick, England. He is a MA in Writing student. He goes to the same cafes. (Timberyard in London, Yaboo in Taipei, Brew Lab in Edinburgh, Must Puudel in Tallinn, etc.) He chooses the same corners to sit. He crunches the same flavours of crisps. But when he does something different, you know it's going to be very different. Like he bought a ticket to Bulgaria. Last summer he was in Taiwan. That's where he is from. This summer he is still not sure where to be.

Debra Bonier

I am currently a student at the University of Houston Clear Lake, majoring in Interdisciplinary Studies. I live in Webster, Texas with my daughter Aneika, son Shaun, and a mix-breed puppy named Teddy. My dream job is to be a writer... but that is another chapter.

E. M. Cooper

My name is E.M. Cooper and I am from the Puget Sound region in Washington State. Writing is a personal hobby of mine and I like sharing my works with others. I hope to improve myself so that I can become a better writer and that my works can be an enjoyable experience to those that read them.

Fabio Sassi

Fabio Sassi started making visual artworks after varied experiences in music and writing. He makes acrylics with the stencil technique on board, canvas, or other media. He uses logos, tiny objects and what is hidden, discarded or considered to have no worth by the mainstream. He still prefers to shoot with an analog camera. Fabio lives and works in Bologna, Italy. His work can be viewed at www.fabiosassi.foliohd.com

Grace Mack

My name is Grace, I am a senior in high school, and my dream is to be a National Geographic photographer. I have been taking photos for three years now. It is my PASSION!!

Hannah Gordon

Hannah Gordon is an aspiring fiction writer who got her first taste of writing when her parents bought her a Harry Potter themed journal that she carried everywhere with her at the age of nine. She eventually lost said Harry Potter themed journal, but she never lost the need to write stories more interesting than her own life. Among other things, Hannah is a cat lover, a comedian (in her own opinion), and a compulsive coffee drinker.

J. J. Steinfeld

J. J. Steinfeld is a Canadian fiction writer, poet, and playwright who lives on Prince Edward Island, where he is patiently waiting for Godot's arrival and a phone call from Kafka. While waiting, he has published fourteen books, including Should the Word Hell Be Capitalized? (Stories, Gaspereau Press), Would You Hide Me? (Stories, Gaspereau Press), An Affection for Precipices (Poetry, Serengeti Press), Misshapenness (Poetry, Ekstasis Editions), and A Glass Shard and Memory (Stories, Recliner Books). His short stories and poems have appeared in numerous anthologies and periodicals internationally, and over forty of his one-act plays and a handful of full-length plays have been performed in Canada and the United States.

Jane Hertenstein

Jane Hertenstein's current obsession is flash. She is the author of over 40 published stories, a combination of fiction, creative non-fiction, and blurred genre both micro and macro. In addition she has published a YA novel, Beyond Paradise, and a non-fiction project, Orphan Girl: T he Memoir of a Chicago Bag Lady, which garnered national reviews. She is a 2x recipient of a grant from the Illinois Arts Council. Her work has appeared or is forthcoming in: Hunger Mountain, Rosebud, Word Riot, Flashquake, Fiction Fix, Frostwriting, and several themed anthologies. She can be found at http://memoirouswrite.blogspot.com/. Her latest book is Freeze Frame: How To Write Flash Memoir.

Jessi Schultz

My name is Jessi Schultz, and I am a writer in love with seeing the world at many different angles. Living in Hawaii has it's perks, especially for a naturalist poet. Many predicaments led to where I am currently in life. College began as a way to appease my parents. It developed as a way to expose myself to fine literature from way back when to current Hawaiian themes and ones abroad. I have not yet learned enough about my craft. I will not stop writing to live what my parents deem a "normal life."

John Hunchak

My name is John Hunchak, I am a 19 year old Arts student at the University of Alberta. I have previously published a story titled "Avocado" in Black Heart Magazine.

John Grey

John Grey is an Australian born poet. Recently published in International Poetry Review, Vallum and the science fiction anthology, "T he Kennedy Curse" with work upcoming in Bryant Literary Magazine, Natural Bridge and the Pedestal.

Kai James

I do art for fun in Boulder, Colorado where I attend graduate school at Naropa. My favorite medium is ink and marker.

Karen Boissonneault-Gauthier

Karen Boissonneault-Gauthier is a French Canadian Métis with more than 20 years writing and photography experience. Her works have been published in national and regional papers, vocational journals and heritage museums. With degrees in Journalism and Mass Communications as well as Photography, she's written and photographed everything from news, fashion, lifestyle and business to sports events. To see more of Karen's photography, visit Zen Dixie Magazine, Dactyl, Cactus Heart Press, Vagabonds Anthology Vol. 2 and Crack T he Spine Literary Magazine, to name but few journals where her work is featured inside and on covers.

Kat Lewis

An alchemist of semantics, Kat Lewis transmutes graphemes and phonemes into tales that chronicle human frailty. An author of four novels and two feature length screenplays, she finds herself a slave to words and their meanings. When she isn't writing or rewriting, Lewis directs short films and pursues a degree in Writing Seminars at The Johns Hopkins University.

Kayla Conway

Kayla Conway is currently a student at Salem College double majoring in English and Creative Writing. She is pursuing a career in journalism. Her work has won first place in her county's art council's annual literary competition.

Kieran

Kieran O'Mant writes poetry when he can and isn't working on his debut novel about a very old man who isn't very nice. He maintains a blog for poetry and short stories which traces out his embarrassingly slow progress to becoming a writer. It is found at http://kieranwritesthingssometimes.blogspot.co.uk/ and updates itself maybe twice a year, if he remembers to.

Laura Kitzmiller

Laura lives in Boulder, CO and is a graduate student at Naropa University in the Contemplative Psychotherapy program. She graduated in 2010 from the University of Kansas with a Bachelor's degree in Creative Writing. She has published her own chapbook, Landmarks, and has also been previously published in the poetry journal Blue Island Review.

Loren Kantor

Loren Kantor is a Los Angeles based woodcut artist. He carves original images of his favorite cultural icons from the past and present.

Morgan Christie

A Toronto, ON native, Morgan Christie travelled well south of the border to pursuit her BA in Creative Writing. Morgan was recently awarded the Katherine B. Rondthaler Award for Prose and a President's Prize in Creative Writing. She's been told she likes to live on the edge and has been called a 'Mad One' from time to time; therefore, felt right at home at Vagabonds. She plans to attend graduate school and obtain an MFA in Creative Writing. Her flash fiction has appeared in, and can be found at, hippocampusmagazine.com.

Phil Lane

Phil Lane's poems, stories and flash fiction have been appearing intermittently online and in print for the past decade approximately. Mr. Lane, a Boston Terrier and Bob Dylan enthusiast, lives in New Jersey and teaches English for a private tutoring company. He can be found online at twitter.com/thephillane

Regina Murray Brault

Regina Murray Brault has twice been nominated for the Push Cart Prize. Her poems have appeared in more than 150 different anthologies, magazines, chapbooks, journals and newspapers, such as Comstock Review, Anthology of New England Writers, AARP Magazine, Great American Poetry Show, Inkwell Magazine and Poet Magazine.

Sendokidu

Sendokidu Adomi is but a budding writer of three years. Always fascinated with the arts, he took up writing as an interest and a challenge. His work stems from a more archaic age, focusing on lush imagery and stories. Sendokidu wishes to bring about the old form of writing, to illustrate the world and dreams that come with it.

Simon Hibberd

What a daunting thing to write, a biography?!!
I was born in Coventry in 1985, England and I know hold up in Colchester these days. I have written my whole life and in the last few years whilst doing an English literature degree it has become my daily routine

Steve De France

Steve De France is a widely published poet, playwright and essayist both in America and in Great Britain. His work has appeared in literary publications in America, England, Canada, France, Ireland, Wales, Scotland, India, Australia, and New Zealand. He has been nominated for a Pushcart Prize in Poetry in 2002, 2003 & 2006. Recently, his work has appeared in The Wallace Stevens Journal, The Mid-American Poetry Review, Ambit, Atlantic, Clean Sheets, Poetry Bay, The Yellow Medicine Review and The Sun. In England he won a Reader's Award in Orbis Magazine for his poem "Hawks." In the United States he won the Josh Samuels' Annual Poetry Competition (2003) for his poem: "The Man Who Loved Mermaids." His play THE KILLER had it's world premier at the GARAGE THEATER in Long Beach, California (Sept-October 2006). He has received the Distinguished Alumnus Award from Chapman University for his writing. Most recently his poem "Gregor's Wings" has been nominated for T he Best of The Net by Poetic Diversity.

Valentina Cano

Valentina Cano is a student of classical singing who spends whatever free time either writing or reading. Her works have appeared in Exercise Bowler, Blinking Cursor, Theory Train, Cartier Street Press, Berg Gasse 19, Precious Metals, A Handful of Dust, The Scarlet Sound, The Adroit Journal, Perceptions Literary Magazine, Welcome to Wherever, The Corner Club Press, Death Rattle, Danse Macabre, Subliminal Interiors, Generations Literary Journal, A Narrow Fellow, Super Poetry Highway, Stream Press, Stone Telling, Popshot, Golden Sparrow Literary Review, Rem Magazine, Structo, The 22 Magazine, The Black Fox Literary Magazine, Niteblade, Tuck Magazine, Ontologica, Congruent Spaces Magazine, Pipe Dream, Decades Review, Anatomy, Lowest of Chronicle, Muddy River

Poetry Review, Lady Ink Magazine, Spark Anthology, Awaken Consciousness Magazine, Vine Leaves Literary Magazine, Avalon Literary Review, Caduceus, White Masquerade Anthology and Perhaps I'm Wrong About the World. Her poetry has been nominated for Best of the Web and the Pushcart Prize. Her debut novel, The Rose Master, will be published in 2014. You can find her here: http://carabosseslibrary.blogspot.com

William S. Tribell

William S. Tribell is an American poet. After years of constant travel and living abroad he has recently returned to the United States. His work appears in journals and magazines around the world and William currently hosts a live radio show called Spectrum on 91.3 fm the Gap. His favorite color is green and he likes sushi.

Vagabonds Crossword Search

```
X  Q  D  M  A  T  G  G  L  Z  Y  Y  B  U  E  A  N  X  T  L
W  F  H  E  L  A  N  O  P  H  E  G  N  N  S  T  O  Z  X  E
S  Y  L  I  L  B  Q  P  Y  R  V  C  B  O  W  Y  S  D  M  F
M  Z  J  G  I  G  F  M  N  I  E  J  Y  R  R  F  O  U  P  P
V  R  A  U  T  Z  X  M  H  J  L  X  L  P  V  I  S  G  Y  I
G  X  P  I  E  F  H  B  J  H  F  R  L  O  M  E  O  J  E  P
H  B  H  N  R  D  X  P  U  V  F  W  D  F  D  D  U  F  F  O
L  F  Y  B  A  D  S  V  Z  P  U  U  Y  J  O  X  J  H  J  R
S  K  R  L  T  Y  R  Q  L  R  F  S  T  P  T  Q  O  F  X  T
Z  J  Y  Z  I  K  K  K  M  U  R  Z  K  A  Z  P  C  I  Q  M
W  Z  D  B  O  L  P  C  W  C  E  T  P  O  H  I  P  D  R  A
M  F  E  E  N  D  Z  E  O  K  K  O  D  S  Y  J  P  X  T  N
M  J  R  Z  K  R  A  K  N  W  S  W  D  U  E  T  L  L  Y  T
K  N  K  A  T  S  U  U  E  I  R  K  W  H  A  F  P  L  E  E
J  C  B  L  E  E  Q  Y  T  S  L  E  S  V  Q  C  P  F  K  A
B  T  Y  L  I  Y  Q  I  V  U  E  N  B  O  S  Q  I  Q  Q  U
A  Y  Q  M  H  C  O  Y  U  O  W  Y  Z  B  I  G  B  W  H  I
N  R  S  N  C  N  X  D  K  R  K  N  R  L  A  S  U  O  R  A
I  I  G  L  N  Z  D  H  H  V  O  K  W  T  X  J  Q  S  R  U
R  A  L  L  U  S  I  O  N  G  W  Q  S  N  Q  T  M  Y  Q  V
W  O  V  P  N  A  K  W  P  F  X  S  Y  L  B  D  P  B  J  K
Q  B  N  S  B  X  G  L  O  X  N  C  E  R  L  W  H  F  F  R
```

What's this?!

It is a cross between a word search and a crossword puzzle!

In the space above there are 15 words for you to find, and on the opposite page are your clues.

Why not loosen up a bit, have some fun, and test your mental mettle and literary savvy.

Enjoy
~Valdon

1.   Title of Allen Ginsberg's most famous work – begins "I saw the best minds of my generation destroyed by madness, starving hysterical naked" (4 letters)

2.   A poetic device ; (noun) 1. a passing or casual reference; an incidental mention of something, either directly or by implication 2. the act or practice of making a casual or indirect reference to something. (8 letters)

3.   (adj) bewildered or confused ; or, more poetically, the state of one who has had the sacred honey dropped upon their tongue by the graces of the nine Goddesses alluded to in the introduction to this issue of Vagabonds (7 letters)

4.   The founder and chief editor of Vagabonds (6 letters)

5.   The journalistic and literary style of Hunter S. Thompson (5 letters)

6.   Full Name of the "hero of the west coast" from Jack Kerouac's Dharma Bums ; based on real life poet Gary Snyder (10 letters)

7.   Last name of the author of One Flew Over the Cuckoo's Nest ; one of the Merry Pranksters (5 letters)

8.   A poetic device ; (noun) the use of the same consonant or of a vowel, not necessarily the same vowel, at the beginning of each word or each stressed syllable in a lie of verse, i.e. crazy cuckoos call in a kerfuffle of commotion (12 letters)

9.   A poetic device ; (noun) 1. the use of words to convey a meaning that is the opposite of its literal meaning 2. An outcome of events contrary to what was, or might have been, expected (5 letters)

10. A poetic device/artistic technique ; (noun) an act or instance of placing close together or side by side, especially for comparison or contrast (13 letters)

11. An underused but quite fanciful and playful word ; (noun) informal chiefly (Brit) commotion; disorder; agitation (9 letters)

12. The beast that was vanquished by the snicker-snack of the Vorpal Sword in Through the Looking-Glass and What Alice Found There ; the name of this poem (11 letters)

13. Last name of Dublin born poet, playwright, and author known for works such as "The Importance of Being Earnest" and The Picture of Dorian Gray (5 letters)

14. (n) a noisy or drunken feast or social gathering; revelry (8 letters)

15. A literary/linguistic device ; (n) a combination of words or morphemes, and their definitions, into one new word ; a word that fuses both the sounds and the meanings of its components, i.e. slithy, mimsy (11 letters)

Weasel Press

Weasel Press is a new independent publisher still figuring things out in the literary world. We're dedicated in seeking quality writers and helping them get a voice in an already loud world. We're a little rusty at the moment since things are still under construction, but we hope to build a great reputation!

Our first publication was Vagabonds: Anthology of the Mad Ones, a literary magazine that is still printing and still growing. From there we've grown into a few other titles. This past year we've released two issues of Vagabonds, partnered with Mind Steady Productions to bring an electric issue of Open Mind, and dove into the darker world with The Haunted Traveler. We've got a lot of plans for the near future, so stick around and watch us grow into something awesome!

Please view our Current Publications to get a better feel for what we'll be doing in the future! We gladly accept all questions, comments, concerns through email at

systmaticwzl@gmail.com

Weasel Press
Fund Raiser

We're an independent publisher looking at releasing the most dedicated writers and poets. We've got a solid mix of people on our list for the first few releases this year and we'd like to keep pushing forward into a larger scale of publishing. It is our goal to raise awareness for emerging artists and writers.

We have big plans, including a small scale documentary focusing on the "death" of poetry. We're in the process of interviewing several poets and shooting several poetry readings; gathering footage and thoughts on the current state of the poetry world. In short it lives, but not in the manner we'd want it to live in. So we're being proactive and getting more noise for an endangered species.

We want to continue focusing on the topics we enjoy and bring about some of the best writers you'll ever experience. You can help us at our go fund me page below or at the paypal email address listed. If you can't donate financially, Weasel Press is always looking for interested people. To find out other ways you can help just shoot us a message!

Paypal: hitchingpoets@hotmail.com

http://www.gofundme/weaselpress

Made in the USA
Lexington, KY
01 June 2014